AF584685

GOD CARES FOR ME

Helping Children Trust God When They're Sick

SCOTT JAMES

Illustrated by
Trish Mahoney

Give all your worries and cares to God,
for he cares about you.

1 Peter 5:7 NLT

Dear Parent or Caregiver,

I wrote this book because I know how difficult it can be to walk through times of pain and suffering with a sick child. As a pediatrician, I have the great privilege of ministering to children and families in such times of need. Praise God, I am often able to minister through the art of healing and restoration, but whatever the prognosis, my job is to love and care for families who have been brought low into the valley. As a parent, I know what it's like to walk that valley myself.

No matter what the illness, it's hard to watch children suffer. It's scary for them to have to face being sick, but it often leaves those of us caring for them feeling scared and anxious too. We want to provide comfort, but sometimes we struggle to find the right words for these difficult conversations. How can we continue to faithfully point our children to God?

God Cares for Me shows children that even when we are sick, God is right there with us. We can trust him. He loves to take care of his children, and he calls us to imitate him by caring for those around us. Each and every one of us can run to him in times of need, and each of us can be a help to others in their time of need. My hope is that this book will help your family celebrate these foundational truths about the "God of all comfort" (2 Corinthians 1:3) and then springboard you into many rich conversations about how he is with you even when you walk through the valley.

In Christ,
Scott James

One chilly Monday morning,
Lucas woke up with a sore throat.
Everything else hurt too and he was so hot.
He tried to yell, “Mama” from his bed,
but all that came out was a croak.

“Lucas,” Mama shouted from downstairs,
“time to get up and get ready for school.”
Again Lucas tried to talk. Again all he could do was croak.

I sound like a frog,
he thought as he fell back to sleep.

And that's how Mama found him.
She touched his head and said,
"Lucas, you are burning hot!"

Lucas rasped,
"My throat hurts so much. I can hardly talk."

"No school for you! You are going to see Dr. Jenn.
Papa can take you this morning."

Lucas groaned. He didn't like doctors very much.

Papa came in to help Lucas get dressed.

"I don't want to go to the doctor," said Lucas as he burrowed deeper under the covers.

"I know," said Papa, "but God gave us doctors to help keep us safe. And you know Dr. Jenn— you see her in church every Sunday. She just wants to help you get better."

"Lucas, remind me—what verse do we say every night before bed?"

Not even pausing for a second, Lucas said,

**"The name of the Lord is a strong tower;
the righteous run into it and are safe."***

Papa said, "I know you don't feel like running right now, but we *can* ask Jesus to help you. That's what it means to run to him."

Papa prayed,
"Dear Jesus, please help Lucas
not be afraid of going to see Dr. Jenn
and help him to feel better soon. Amen."

Lucas groaned again, but this time he let Papa help him get dressed.

*Proverbs 18:10 (NRSV)

Papa helped Lucas
get in the car, and they
drove to Dr. Jenn's office.

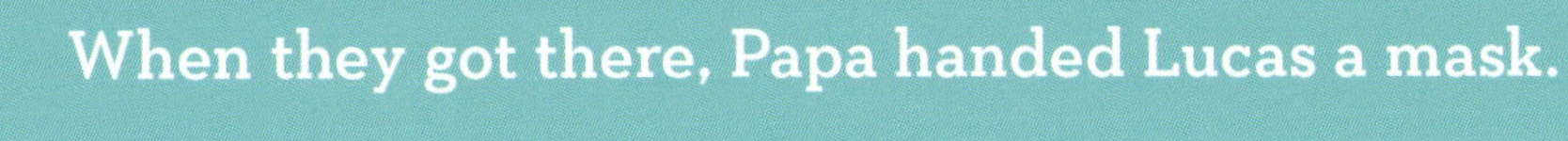

When they got there, Papa handed Lucas a mask.

"Don't forget that we have to mask up," he said. "It's one way we can help keep others safe. We don't want them to get whatever you have."

Lucas and Papa both put on their masks and walked into the doctor's office.

Miss Anne greeted them cheerfully and told them to sit on the left. Lucas knew that's where all the sick kids waited.

"Dr. Jenn will be right with you," Miss Anne said.

Lucas leaned against Papa's shoulder.

His head hurt.
Everything hurt.

A few minutes letter, Nurse Abby brought them back to a small room. She took Lucas's temperature and wrote something down. Then Dr. Jenn came in.

"How are you feeling, Lucas?" she asked.

"I'm fine," he said without really thinking.

Dr. Jenn said, "Lucas, how are you *really* feeling?"

"Not too good. My head hurts. And I can't swallow because my throat hurts so much."

"I'm sorry you are sick, Lucas. We're going to help you feel better."

Dr. Jenn peered down Lucas's throat,

looked into his ears,

listened to him breathe,

and pushed on his tummy.

"Lucas, I think we are going to do a few tests so we can know how to help you get better."

Lucas started to cry.
He didn't feel good and tests sounded scary.

"I know you might be nervous, Lucas," said Dr. Jenn, "but Jesus will help you. Remember what we talked about in church this week?"

"What?" asked Lucas.

"Pastor John said that Jesus cares for us in hard times. The Bible tells us to give all our cares to God because he cares for us.*

Jesus loves to take care of us—
he's like a hen protecting chicks under her wings."**

"And Jesus is a strong tower that we can run to," Lucas added.

* from 1 Peter 5:7
** from Matthew 23:37

Just then Nurse Abby came in with a tray.

She swabbed the back of Lucas's throat. It tickled but it was over quickly.

Then she took some blood.

Lucas looked away. It pinched, but then it was done too.

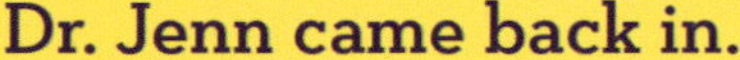

Dr. Jenn came back in.

"Lucas," she said,
"while we wait for your tests to come back,
you'll need to stay home from school."

That was fine with Lucas.
He didn't feel like going to school anyway.

**"Remember," Dr. Jenn continued,
"it's important to look out for the good of others,
even when you're feeling bad yourself."**

"When you're sick, you can help keep others safe by:

1 Washing your hands to keep them clean and germ-free,

2 Staying home until you're feeling better,

3 Wearing a mask to keep your germs to yourself, and

4 Keeping some distance between yourself and others to make it harder for the germs to jump from person to person."

“I remember,” sighed Lucas.
“Mama and Papa remind me
every time I’m sick!

**But when will I be able to
hug Grandma and Grandpa again?**

**And what about my friends?
When can I play with them again?!”**

"I know it's hard," agreed Dr. Jenn. "Sometimes, looking out for others means choosing to do things that aren't fun. Did you know that I have to wear a mask all the time when I'm at work?

It fogs up my glasses,

and at the end of the day my nose hurts so much—it's annoying!

But I do it to keep others safe. The Bible says, 'Love does no harm to a neighbor.'"*

"Okay," said Lucas. All of a sudden he wanted to go home. His head hurt.

* Romans 13:10 (NIV)

Dr. Jenn handed Papa a list of instructions and a prescription for Lucas.

Then she said, “Get some rest, Lucas. Before you know it, you will be feeling better.”

Lucas sure hoped so.

As Dr. Jenn smiled and waved good-bye, she reminded Lucas,

"God LOVES to take care of you,

and

you can help care for others, too."

Papa helped Lucas get into the car.

As they drove home, Lucas thought about what Dr. Jenn had said. "Is everyone my neighbor?" Lucas asked.

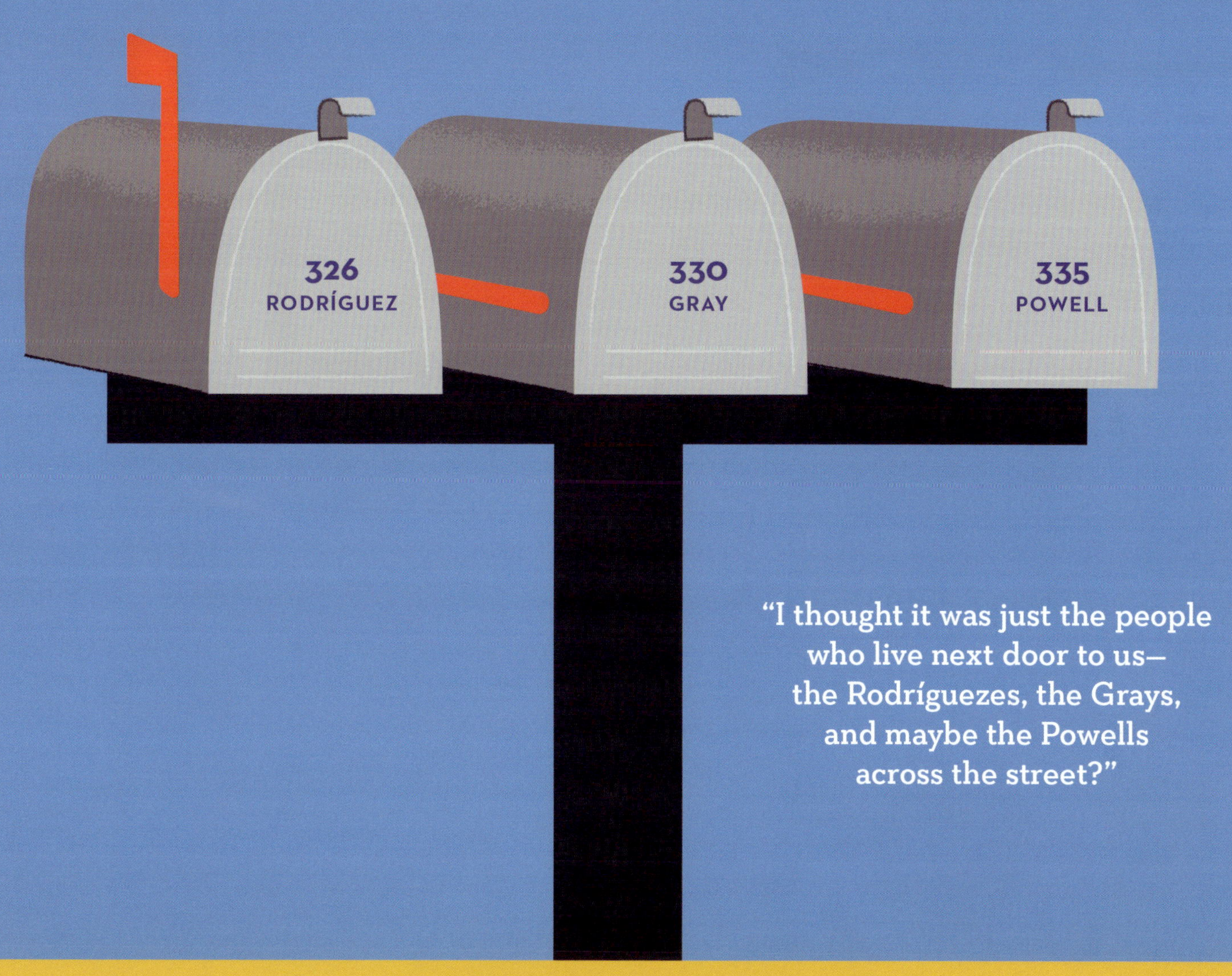

"I thought it was just the people who live next door to us— the Rodríguezes, the Grays, and maybe the Powells across the street?"

"Well," said Papa, "God also says in the Bible, 'The Lord is good to all, and his mercy is over all that he has made.'*

'All' means everyone.
Since God is good to all, we should be too."

* Psalm 145:9

When they got home, Lucas curled up on the couch under a blanket and watched a movie.

Papa went into the kitchen and started to make his famous chicken soup.

Whenever he made it for people who weren't feeling well, Papa always said,

"My chicken soup will cure what ails you!"

So, of course, he said it as he brought it in to Lucas. Lucas groaned, but he really was hoping that was true.

Just then there was a knock at the front door.

knock
knock

Lucas looked out the window and saw his grandparents waiting on the front step.

"Papa," he croaked, "Grandma and Grandpa are here!"

Lucas didn't know what to do. He wanted to give them a hug, but he didn't want them to get sick. He remembered what Dr. Jenn had said about keeping others safe.

Papa put his mask on and opened the front door. He stood back a few feet as he greeted his parents.

That must be hard for Papa, Lucas thought as he watched.

Papa told them, "I wish you could come in, but Lucas is sick."

"Oh no!" said Grandma and Grandpa at the same time. They waved to Lucas from the front steps.

"We don't want you to get sick too," said Papa.

"Me neither!" said Grandpa. "We can come back when he's feeling better."

"Lucas, make sure you eat all of your Papa's chicken soup and drink lots of water," Grandma called.

"We love you!"

"We'll let you know when it's safe for you to visit again," said Papa as he waved good-bye.

That night as Mama
tucked him into bed,
Lucas told her all
about his day—

the throat swab,
the pinch when they took his blood,
the talk with Dr. Jenn about
keeping other people safe—
and then not being able to give
Grandma and Grandpa a hug.

"That's a lot," said Mama. "How are you feeling now?"

"I feel better," said Lucas. "But when my head hurts, I get a little scared. And I got a little scared for Grandma and Grandpa too. They are old! I don't want anything to happen to them."

"We don't want anyone else to get sick either," agreed Mama. "That's why we're following Dr. Jenn's advice about keeping others safe. Still, I know it can be scary when you're sick.

"Whenever I'm scared or worried, I like to pray God's Word back to him. I tell God,

'When I am afraid, I will trust in you.'*

Lucas, whether we feel sick or well, when we are happy and when we are sad, one thing is always true: God is with us.

"If you ever need a reminder of that, just think about what Jesus did for us. Because Jesus died for our sins and rose again, we can be sure that no matter what happens, he will always be near.

"Another Bible verse that always helps me is,

'Do not fear, for I am with you; do not be afraid, for I am your God. I will strengthen you; I will help you.'**

Lucas, never forget that Jesus is right here with us.

"Do not fear, Jesus is near," Mama whispered softly as Lucas closed his eyes and drifted off to sleep.

* Psalm 56:3 (CSB)
** Isaiah 41:10 (CSB)

Talking with Kids about

SICKNESS

My prayer is that this book would serve as a simple and relatable story to help you teach your children that God is with us, even when things don't seem to be going well. Even if they haven't faced a serious illness, most children have experienced enough to know the kind of frustration and fear Lucas was going through when he felt sick. It's enough to raise big questions in their little hearts, and we have the privilege of shepherding them through it. Still, because suffering and sadness are often involved, this can be a daunting task.

All of this can lead to some very difficult conversations with our children—conversations I hope we are willing to have, for their sake. Perhaps Lucas's story will help you take the next step in that direction. As you do, here are a few suggestions for how to talk with your children about sickness.

1 Acknowledge the hardship.

Children are more perceptive than we give them credit for. When they are facing a difficult illness, there's no point in trying to sugarcoat it. Communicate in kid-friendly ways, yes. Comfort and console them, absolutely. But don't dismiss the hard reality of what they're going through. They know better. They know that pain, suffering, and death exist in this world, and we would be doing them a disservice if we pretended otherwise. So, whether it's their own illness or someone else's that you're talking about with them, go ahead and acknowledge the difficult truth of the situation. But then, help them see how honestly acknowledging this sad reality reveals something they already know to be true: *This is not the way it's meant to be*. The Bible tells us that "sin entered the world through one man, and death through sin, and in this way death came to all people, because all sinned" (Romans 5:12 NIV). Sin has broken this world, bringing sickness and death with it. This is a painful truth, but one that must be acknowledged.

2 Put them on a firm foundation.

Even (especially!) in the middle of the hardship, we get to encourage our children to rest on the bedrock truths that God is in control and he cares for us deeply. "Every word of God proves true; he is a shield to those who take refuge in him" (Proverbs 30:5). The affliction is real, but it does not go unchecked. God is still on his throne, ordaining all things—yes, even illness—for our good and his glory. This may be hard to appreciate as we walk through the valley, but there is comfort in knowing that the Lord is our guiding Shepherd (Psalm 23). He is not baffled by pandemics or cancer diagnoses; he has already defeated death and has green pastures in store for us. Beckon your children to the trustworthy shelter of God our refuge and our fortress (Psalm 91:2).

3 Help them see they're part of a bigger community.

When hard times come, it's helpful to know we're not alone. Through faith in Jesus, we enter into a great big family called the church. Within this family, God surrounds us with people who love us and want to help us through the trials that sickness brings. In fact, this is exactly what the church is called to do—we bear one another's burdens (Galatians 6:2). But the church's love is not just an inward facing love; as we love one another, we also demonstrate God's love to a watching world (John 13:35). In this sense, our community expands to include everyone around us.

We can trust God to care for us—personally, as well as through his church—but we also have the privilege of being used by him to care for those around us. Encourage your children to think about how we can seek the good of our neighbor (1 Corinthians 10:24). Doing our part to love and care for others is a great way to "pursue what makes for peace and for mutual upbuilding" (Romans 14:19).

This book is dedicated to my kids,
Will, Kirstine, Benjamin, and Bethan.

Valleys will certainly come, but you will never have to walk them alone.

New Growth Press, Greensboro, NC 27404

Art and Design: Trish Mahoney

ISBN: 978-1-64507-192-1

Library of Congress Cataloging-in-Publication Data on file

Printed in Canada

28 27 26 25 24 23 22 21 1 2 3 4 5